Hey, little reader!

Today as a team we started a heartfelt adventure.

Did you know that we all have different feelings?

Sometimes we're joyful laughers, and other times we feel nervous.

But don't worry, emotions are like magical colors that paint our hearts!

Chapter 1

Joyful feelings

Hey, have you ever heard of happiness?

Happiness is a feeling that makes you feel like dancing or laughing.

It can happen when you get a gift, spend time with friends or discover something else.

Can you laugh out loud?

Haha!

Now get ready for an exciting
adventure in search of the
rainbow!

When you're feeling happy,
you can create colorful pictures
or watch the clouds and guess
what they represent.

Remember that happiness is
like the sun that shines every
day.

Chapter 2

Unhappy feelings

Sometimes you can feel sad, and this is perfectly normal.

Sadness is a feeling when you expect something, but it doesn't come true.

You may also feel lonely or worried.

Have you ever shed tears when something sad happened?

But you don't have to worry,
little friend!

When you feel depressed, you
can ask an adult to give you a
hug or listen to your favorite
song to make you feel better.

Sadness is similar to rain, but
always remember that it also
brings a rainbow!

Chapter 3

Let's discover
different feelings.

Besides happiness and sadness, there are more feelings for us to explore.

Have you ever experienced fear?

Feeling uncertain or scared of something can make us feel afraid.

It might be darkness, loud sounds, or spiders.

Just remember, if you ever feel scared, you can always ask a grown-up for assistance.

What about being angry?

Anger is a feeling that happens when something makes us mad or upset.

This might occur if someone takes our toys or interrupts us while we are doing something.

However, we can show our anger in positive ways, like:

Saying "I'm upset" or proposing a different game.

Chapter 4

Feelings are similar to the shades of our heart.

Hey there, little readers, did you know?

Feelings are similar to the hues that color our hearts.

At times we blush with joy, and other times we feel blue with sadness.

But what really matters is that all emotions are important, and there is always something to learn from them.

Now that you know about various feelings, you can discuss your emotions with a grown-up.

Just remember, they're always here to assist you.

Don't forget that feelings are a natural part of you, and you can discover how to manage them in positive ways.

Conclusion

That's the end of our book about
feelings.

I hope yoau've discovered more
about your feelings and how to
express them on this journey.

You can feel happy, sad, scared,
or angry - it's all okay!

Now little reader!

Go on your own emotional
journey and try to create a
beautiful image of yourself
with your feelings!

Enjoy your journey.